Breaking Free..

Becoming the single mum to   a
journey into personal developm
development of Vivienne.

A lover of learning, that during her years at school hit peaks and
troughs, has enabled Vivienne to gain a number of qualifications
and accreditations, most notably as a Clinical Hypnotherapist and
Psychotherapist, a Neuro-Linguistic Programming Master
Practitioner, Time Line Therapist and Personal Performance
Coach.

Utilising these and other skills inside a blended, approach,
Vivienne brings focussed transformation programmes to her face
to face and online group workshops, bespoke packages to her 1:1
clients and exclusive and luxury retreats to those who prefer to
get away from it all and indulge themselves in immersive, reset
opportunities.

Previous clients have said:
'I was very skeptical at first but after a few sessions I feel more confident, relaxed and empowered.'
'Vivienne has helped me become the person I've always wanted to be.'
'Through hypnosis, Vivienne has helped me so much with my confidence and self-acceptance. She has enabled me to live my life more freely.'

Recently Vivienne has featured as a panellist at Shaa Wasmund MBE National Women's Conference, been interviewed and Co-Hosted a live Anxiety and Mental Health show on BBC Radio, featured as the guest on several Podcast shows, Co-Authored a Bestselling Book and presented training at the Great Yorkshire Showground Wonderful World of Wellbeing Event together with other local and national personal development, education and business events.

With a background of over thirty years in mainstream and special education, both as a member of senior leadership teams, classroom practitioner and leadership trainer and facilitator, Vivienne blends her knowledge of working in highly pressured results-driven environments together with her in-depth knowledge of the creation of identity, and the freedom we can experience when we explore what is possible outside the limitations that the past has imposed on us.

In her free time Vivienne enjoys travelling at home and abroad, clocking thousands of miles onto her milometer, dancing under the stars, swimming in the sea, upcycling tattered treasures in creative ways, indulging in delicious food, spending time with her family, and is happiest when she is based close to the sea on sunny, hot days.

To connect with Vivienne, you can find her at

www.viviennerawnsley.com

viv@viviennerawnsley.com

@viviennerawnsley

Contents

Introduction

This book is for each of you who at some stage of your life find yourself in a place where you didn't expect to be. For me it was the father of my 5 young sons leaving and my world as I knew it ending.

After every ending there is a new beginning…

My ending started the journey of discovering me.

Through this book I share experiences, together with well used tools that you can dip into and use as the need arises. Along with the offer for you to contact me to explore how working together could further progress your journey into discovering you. And beyond.

The path of self discovery has twists and turns along the way, sometimes with huge potholes to negotiate. The strategies in this book will support you on your travels making the time pass more quickly and smoothly., resulting in new found wealth and opportunity of choices.

Enjoy your journey together with the freedom of choice and wealth of opportunities that breaking free … reclaiming you can bring.

Part 1

"No, I don't love you and I haven't for some time."

My heart thudded in my chest like it never had before as I stared at my husband's emotionless face. Was I hearing right? No. I mustn't have woken up properly yet. Whilst I'd known things hadn't been perfect, what relationship is? I hadn't had any clue that his love for me had gone. And just like that, he was gone. He left behind 17 years of marriage just like that.

I spent the whole day ironing, a task that I hate. Over the duration of that weekend, I lost over half a stone in weight. What was I going to do? Divorce was something that happened to other people, not me! I had five little boys that needed a mum and dad together in a loving home. My entire world had fallen apart in one day.

All I could think about was how I was going to fix it?

Until that moment I had always believed I could fix anything; from saving the runt of the rabbit litter by feeding it with milk from my finger all night, to rescuing my sister from bullies by having a fight with a girl and ending up with my black coat being strewn with copious amounts of my detached blonde tresses.

I had to be able to fix this too.

> **"If it ends bad,
> it doesn't
> mean
> It was
> worthless!"**
>
> Jos Berkemeijer

I lost even more weight, had my hair cut into a new trendy style, wore the most alluring clothing and even went out to buy the latest in wedge heeled shoes to make my legs look longer but with no avail.

He had met someone new, and no amount of effort on my part would get him to come home and try again.
My self-esteem was at an all-time low.
For the first time, I felt I didn't know who I was or where I was heading and I was overwhelmed with a sense of failure.

From this episode in my life, I went on a mission to prove to myself, and the world that I was good enough. I registered on a couple of dating sites, driving up and down the length of Britain to meet around 80 random strangers in motorway services, pubs, and restaurants to fulfil my quest. I was trying to boost my self-esteem but this ultimately left me feeling empty and further rejected.

Attending dance classes 4 or 5 times a week and joining a scuba diving training club were other hobbies I engaged in to prove that I was acceptable and that I was enough. Constantly hoping that the affirmation from others would fill that void inside. Although I became an accomplished dancer and qualified in scuba diving, it was still not enough.

"Kinda Pointless to Fight for what you want

When what you want continues to Break you Heart."

Molly McAdams

I set up a business that after a successful launch, failed.
I know now this was because I undervalued myself and gave a low entry price to those who were struggling financially.
More failure for me to swallow.
Another drop in my self-esteem.

I had to carry on moving forward though as I had my five sons to keep going for.

In an attempt to maintain the lifestyle, they had grown accustomed to, I took my sons on ski holidays that were way outside my tax credit budget and so the search to being complete and whole again continued.

Life had challenges, but I never gave up trying to make it better. I was always looking for a solution, a way to feel better, to feel truly happy and at peace.

Then one day, whilst in the shopping area at Manchester airport, I came across two books that sparked my interest, Fiona Harold's 'Be Your Own Life Coach' and Ken Robinson's 'Finding your Element: How to Discover Your Talents and Passions and Change your Life.'
Lying on a sunbed in Tenerife, I read these books and was inspired to embark upon the next chapter of my life.

> "The Magic
> in
> New Beginnings
>
> Is truly the most
> Powerful of
> them all."
>
> Josiyah Martin

I enrolled in a Personal Performance Coaching training and an NLP course. I believed I was on my way, the courses were going to fix me, and make me whole and complete again.

I excelled in the courses and passed with flying colours yet I didn't feel any better about myself. On the inside, the feeling of unworthiness remained. So my journey into personal development continued for several years, me spending days on end and weekends away from home, thousands of pounds and hundreds of hours doing course after course trying to find that part of me that was missing. Searching for the person who could fix and fill that need inside me.

Years later, with a plethora of knowledge and certificates to prove I was good enough, I realised that no external source was going to fill the void I had deep within me. It was like a light bulb suddenly lit up inside my head and I realised I needed to stop searching and actually just be still and connect with myself. I discovered that everything I needed was inside me, that I was enough already.

But where had the story of me come from?

I pondered upon what had happened to me in my life to leave me thinking that I wasn't enough?

Where had the need to prove that I was enough originated?

Was it actually from my divorce or was it from other earlier experiences or incidences in my life?

"We are Defined By the Stories We tell Ourselves."

Tony Robbins

As I reflected, I remembered incidences at home as the big sister when I felt that I hadn't achieved what was expected of me. I remembered times at school when I had felt that I didn't fit in and even when I tried hard to fit in by wearing the same clothes as others did and hanging out with the less 'swotty' group that need to be enough was lacking.

I remembered early feelings of rejection when the boys I fancied never liked me, the ones who did, I felt obligated to be interested in them. I always felt as though I had to seem to be being perfect in order to be enough. The real me just got squashed deeper and deeper inside, squeezing out in rebellious moments and ending up doing seemingly crazy things.

How had this happened?

I was from a 'normal' family with loving parents who worked hard to provide everything they could for me and my sister and brother. We lived in a comfortable home, ate good food – my mum is an awesome cook even though my dad's turkey carcass soup was always questionable- and even had hotel holidays abroad in the days when many people never even left the country, let alone stay in hotels.

I passed the 11+ selection exam and went on to achieve O' levels, A' levels, and a degree so had the credentials to be accepted as intelligent. I had been highly regarded by the Principle and lecturers at college and senior leadership teams in my career in education.
I had given birth to five healthy sons and always maintained a fit and healthy body reducing my weight to my starting point after each pregnancy.

Looking in on my life from the outside, I appeared to be a successful high achiever, yet on the inside, I felt totally unfulfilled

I had got lost in the story that I had created around past events, and the interpretation that I had made of them, that left me in a place of lack, feeling unworthy and not being enough.

It was realising this that made a huge difference to how I feel inside.

The past isn't real.

It's gone and how we choose to recall it is up to us.

"The stories we tell ourselves shape our lives.
They shape who we believe we are,
And this Belief,
Translates into who we Become."

John Assaraf

When I was little I remember my dad telling me bedtime stories at night.

My favourites were the ones that he made up about three mischievous puppies called 'Woof', 'Tuff' and 'Snuff' and the adventures that they got up to.

Each night's stories would be different unless I asked for an adventure being repeated and even then there were adaptations depending on what my dad remembered and what he felt like putting into the story that night.

Sometimes if it was raining outside the story would take place on a rainy day and if it was a birthday so the story would be based around a birthday.

Remembering these stories got me thinking.

What if the experiences in my life I'd remembered, like the stories from long before, were having an impact on how I'd remembered the event or incident?

With the way I was feeling or the things that had been happening at the time and then like a story I'd made it up?

I'd made up who I was based on what I thought I had to be and what I thought others thought of me.

I then realised if I had made it up, I was the author of the story and could rewrite it in a different way.

In fact, I could create my life and the story of my life in any way I chose to.

" The most adventurous
Journey to embark on;
Is the journey to Yourself

Your most exciting thing to
Discover;
I who You really are.

The most Treasured pieces that
you can find;
Are the pieces of You.

The most special portrait you
can Recognise;
Is the portrait of your Soul."

C Joybell C

v i v i e n n e r a w n s l e y . c o m

That point in time began my journey into finding me. I'd had sessions with several counsellors. I engaged in EMDR (Eye Movement Desensitisation Reprogramming), and put a new perspective on elements of my past and removed blame from those who maybe I'd felt had let me down or impacted on me in a negative way in the past.

CBT (Cognitive Behavioural Therapy) group sessions were provided by the local health authority during which I felt that all I was doing was engaging in the challenges that others were dealing with. I even had hypnotherapy and not knowing what to expect or being informed about it prior to the sessions didn't feel I'd experienced it and was left feeling conned.

Now I'm not saying that these are not really useful and well-proven systems that work. For some people, they are very effective and life-changing.

It's important to remember at this point, I am the eldest daughter of three children, I am creative, I am resilient and I like to maintain control over what's going on around me because that gives me a feeling of safety and being ok and will use this to hide out physically or metaphorically when my inner self feels scared or threatened.

So what was I going to do?
How was I going to get out of this vicious circle, the repeating pattern of victimhood and the life that really wasn't working for me in the way that I wanted it to?

"Infuse your life with Action.
Don't wait for it to Happen.
Make it Happen.
Make your own Future.
Make your own Hope.
Make your own Love.
And whatever your beliefs,
Honour your Creator,
Not by passively waiting for Grace
to come down from upon on high,
But by doing what you can to
make Grace Happen...
Yourself,
Right Now,
Right Down Here on Earth."

Bradley Whitford

I needed to start telling myself a different story! I also realised I needed to stop running away from my feelings and face them head-on.

Did you know that the heart, the part of us that feels pain, is stronger than the brain, the most powerful source of electromagnetic energy in the human body, producing the largest rhythmic electromagnetic field of any of the body's organs? In fact that the heart's electrical field is about 100 times greater in amplitude than the electrical activity generated by the brain and 5000 times stronger magnetically?
So if that is true, which scientists say it is, why was I concentrating so much on what was going on in my continuing negative thought patterns?
Why was I not focussing more on my feelings?

Those parts of me that had been dumbed and numbed down so much, that when an assessor from the mental health service asked me how I felt about what was going on, I was unable to answer her. Or more accurately, I wouldn't allow myself that vulnerability because it might hurt too much and rip open the scars that were still tender.

Instead, I talked about my external situation and what other people in my life were doing. If I was to put the past in the past and rewrite my story, then I needed to start doing things in a different way, start acknowledging those feelings that my huge electronic magnetic powerhouse was pulsating into every cell in my body.

So how did I start? What did I do?

"The most
Courageous act

Is still to
Think for
Yourself

Aloud."

Coco Chanel

v i v i e n n e r a w n s l e y . c o m

Nelson Mandela said that "There is no easy walk to freedom anywhere, and many of us will have to pass through the valley of the shadow of death again and again before we reach the mountaintop of our desires."

My first step up my mountain was that I acknowledged where I was at. Instead of looking externally to find the easy route, the usual brave face I put on for myself and anyone else looking in, it was time to explore how I really was, what I felt and the feelings that I wanted to experience rather than those I had created stories around that were expected or allowed.

I had a table filled with certificates that prove my skill set, I had my five boys who grew from those not so tiny babies into men bigger and stronger than me. I had a house over-filled with possessions. A regular income that was always overstretched.

I had attended hundreds of hours and spent thousands of pounds attending personal development, business and speaker training. All of them shouting in loud voices my need for external evidence to prove who I was and yet never really representing the me that is beneath the surface.

I began to realise that unless I looked beneath the superficial and continued to rely on the ability of other to fix me, I would never allow the past to diminish and the essence of me to rise like a phoenix from the ashes.

The next step was creating space.

Space to feel.

A space that removed the noise of the could do, should do, have to.

A space that would allow the desire that was shelved somewhere inside me to grow.

I started to take time for me.

As a full-time teacher, homemaker and carer of 5 boys, the balls I juggled were many and the time I took for me, slim.

"Life isn't about Finding yourself.

Life is about Creating yourself."

George Bernard Shaw

However, I began to take a bath in the morning instead of a shower. To make myself and drink, cups of a wide variety of delicious herbal teas. To download audible books to listen to whilst I was driving in the car. I created opportunities to explore where I was at, what I was actually enjoying. What I was feeling satisfied with and what was adding to the pressure and burdens of the day.

And as I felt, something amazing happened. I began to explore the reality of my life, the facts about what really existed, versus the stories that I had created way back when. I didn't even have origins for many of them, just vague recollections of how it might have been and from the interpretations I'd made in my formative years. This explained how my perceived identity had been born.

The eldest daughter. I knew what it was like for me when I had my first son, that unknown realm of parenthood. How did I do it? Would someone come and take him from me now I'd done the carrying him for 9+ months and given birth to him. Surely, I wasn't going to be trusted with this tiny human being?

What had it been like for my parents?

How had it been being the eldest of three children?

When had things been said in fun and not, that I'd taken to heart and made my reality?

What events had taken place that I had made my own interpretation about? Where I'd created who I was, what I was worth and capable of?

Why would my creative imagination have been any less vivid then?

I remembered being at school and being asked to write a story, being given the title and then being allowed to write whatever I wanted. If I could write whatever I wanted then what was so different about now? Was it possible that when I woke up in the morning, rather than the day taking charge of the way I felt and the things I accomplished, I could design the day and the way I felt?

Better still, could I create a plan from the things I wanted to accomplish, to support the way I wanted to feel and fit them around the things that were expected of me? And could I even explore those things that were expected of me? Were they really expected of me or had I made those boundaries too? And if I had made them, then I could then also, unmake or alter them? Just like the eraser in my pencil case when I was at school, I could rub out the parts of my life and the parts of me that were leaving me with negative feelings and rewrite my story and create a new plan for my life moving forward.

"It is a
Beautiful New
Chapter
in this
Book we call Life".
Write it.
Live it. Create it.
Every Day.
But most Importantly
Liberate it."

Angela Gwinner

viviennerawnsley.com

It was at this point that I revisited hypnotherapy, however this time as a practitioner rather than as a client. I learned about the power of the subconscious mind, and that how although logically and cognitively I could know about all the memories, thoughts and feelings I wanted to rub out, alter and change, part of me kept holding on tightly not letting go and allowing me to transform my life.

My subconscious mind. The part of me that has always been awake, always been working hard to keep me alive and keep me safe. Storing the memories and events of the past as a reminder of what is dangerous and what is safe and how I must behave accordingly.

Through my period of training, I was always the person to volunteer for any new technique or process to be demonstrated and practiced with 'clients' between training sessions. As I continued being the subject of hypnosis and using hypnosis with others I started to notice changes taking place.

My subconscious letting go of the patterns of the past and rebooting with programmes that allow me freedom and choice. Ways that I would have reacted to situations previously being different, things that would have upset, disturbed or angered me in the past having little or no effect. My feelings around situations of the past were diminished.

Transformation was taking place.

> "It's not about Perfect,
> It's about Effort.
> And when you Implement
> that Effort into your Life.
> Every single day,
> That's where
> Transformation happens.
> That's how Change occurs.
> Keep going.
> Remember why you
> started."
>
> Anonymous

This continued over time, creating the space I desired to start doing things differently, having the opportunity to choose how I react and instead respond to situations. The old thought patterns of the past no-longer taking charge. Allowing me the space to acknowledge my feelings about situations and make choices rather than living on auto-pilot.

Clients too began to notice deep and profound changes taking place in their lives. Those who had suffered from the feelings of depression for most of their lives, recognising that the feelings had lifted. Leaving them with good and not so good days but no longer feeling depressed.

Other clients overcame feelings of anxiety that had been created in their formative years. Leaving them enjoying newfound confidence and ability to communicate effectively with others, create relationship and make career choices that would have previously seemed impossible.

The impact of the use of hypnosis blended with the other skills I have developed over the years was creating tangible differences in my life and the lives of those I worked with.

One client worked through the limiting physical conditions of fibromyalgia, underactive thyroid and diabetes. She also overcame the emotional limiting beliefs of not being worthy and not being good enough resulting in her being able to lose over four stone in weight. This meant she achieved her goal of having knee replacements so she could go for long walks in the countryside once more. Another client conquered their stories, fears and limiting beliefs to being appointed in the job of their dreams. Many clients de-cluttered and discarded emotional as well as physical baggage that they no-longer-needed or felt was necessary for them to hold onto. Other clients overcame limiting beliefs which had held them back in developing their businesses, resulting in the freedom of choice and enabling them to make the changes that they needed to take their lives to the next level.

So my life began to change. I began to make new choices. No longer feeling the need to please others because I was the big sister, the wife, the x-wife, the mother ... but being free to choose, free to write my story in whichever and whatever way I chose. Creating a successful business that supports others in recognising the stories that they tell themselves, changing stories and transforming lives.

"You and I possess within ourselves at every moment of our lives,

Under all Circumstances,

The Power to Transform the Quality of our lives."

Werner Erhard

viviennerawnsley.com

It's interesting that I find myself sitting writing this account in the same place that my journey began, in Tenerife. Another of those opportunities that would never have happened without the changes that have taken place in me.

In the words of Rumi, 'What you seek, is seeking you.'

Once upon a time, there lived a girl called Cinderella...

And the beautiful princess lived happily ever after.

The End or ...
the Start of Another Beginning

Part 2

Simple Self Soothe Strategies

These strategies can be adapted and used to become your SOS survival kit.

Self Soothing Comfort Box or Bag

Create yourself a personal 'go to' self-soothing box or bag.

Carefully choose the items to put inside that will support you when the need arises.

These may include:

◊ An aromatherapy wheat bag that can be warmed
◊ Stress ball
◊ Anti anxiety calming prompt card
◊ Headache tablets
◊ Aromatherapy playdough or moulding clay
◊ Colouring book and pencils/ felt tips
◊ Sleeping mask
◊ Scented candle
◊ Comforting smells
◊ Music playlist
◊ Guided meditation
◊ Soft things
◊ Pictures of loved ones
◊ Sachet of hot chocolate or favourite herbal tea
◊ Snuggly jumper or blanket
◊ Favourite essential oils
◊ Massage creams and lotions

Add to the list things that are important, special and comforting

Use it and if it doesn't work for you lose it.

First practice each of these strategies during a time when you are feeling calm, relaxed and in control.

Massage

⇒ Find some lotion or cream with a texture and scent that you like.
⇒ Massage your hands.
⇒ Experience the touch, the smell as you massage kindness and balance into your body.
⇒ As you massage your hands take any tensions or worries towards your fingertips then massage them away.

Looking Inwards

⇒ Close your eyes and look inwards
⇒ Cut out all incoming information.
⇒ Close your eyes and take a deep breath.
⇒ Look inwards.
⇒ Sit still for 30 seconds.
⇒ Allow your breath to slowly exhale.

Give yourself a hug

⇒ Wrap your arms around yourself and give you a hug.
⇒ Use a blanket or a duvet to deepen the pressure and intensify the hug.
⇒ Whilst you're hugging yourself use some of the mantras and affirmations that you have chosen to increase the feeling of being held both physically and emotionally.

Butterfly Hug

Developed by Lucina Artigas, M.A. in her work with survivors of the Acapulco Hurricane of 1997, the butterfly hug is a wonderful way to get your focus back to your body when you are experiencing strong emotion. It also works after the fact to release emotions associated with a painful or undesirable memory.

Here's how to do it:

⇒ Think of a memory you would like to lessen the emotion associated with. Rate the strength of your feelings on a scale of 1 to 10.
⇒ Cross your arms in front of your chest with the tips of the fingers of each hand resting just below the clavicle on each side.
⇒ Gently close your eyes or look softly down.
⇒ Alternate gentle tapping on each side (It kind of looks like the flutter of butterfly wings, hence the name)
⇒ Breathe deep and slow while you are gently alternating the tapping. Tap for about 3 minutes.
⇒ Now think of the feeling associated with the memory and rate it again. See if it feels weaker this time when you think about it.
⇒ Repeat.

Box breathing

⇒ Take control and create a mindful moment as your breathing forms a square.
⇒ Breathe in for the count of 4.
⇒ Hold your breath in for the count of 4.
⇒ Breathe out for the count of 4.
⇒ Hold your breath out for the count of 4.

The length can be increased from 4 to 8 as your capacity to breathe in this way increases.

Body Scan

Three-minute breathing space for when your thoughts or mood start to spiral in a negative direction that you can record and use whenever or whenever you choose to.

⇒ The **first step** is to take a definite posture so that you move into the present moment quickly.
⇒ Your back is erect, but not stiff, letting the body express a sense of being present and awake.

⇒ Now, closing your, eyes, if it feels comfortable, take the first step of becoming aware of what is going on with you right now.
⇒ Becoming conscious of what is going through your mind: what thoughts are around?

⇒ Here again, as best as you can, just noting thoughts as mental events... so we note them, and then we note the feelings that are around at the moment... in particular, turning them toward any sense of discomfort or unpleasant feelings.

⇒ So rather than try to push them away or shut them out, perhaps saying, 'Ah there you are; that's how it is right now.'
⇒ Similarly, with sensations in the body... are there sensations of tensions, of holding, of letting go?
⇒ And again, becoming aware of them, simply noting whatever is arising in this moment.

Silence (15 seconds)

⇒ So, you have a sense of what is going on right now, having stepped out of automatic pilot.

⇒ The **second step** is to collect your awareness by focussing on a single act-the movement of the breath.

⇒ So really gather yourself, focussing your attention down in the movements of the abdomen, the rise and fall of the belly as the breath moves in and out... spending a minute or so to focus on the motion of the abdominal wall, moment by moment, breath by breath, as best as you can right here, right now. Noticing when the breath is moving in and when the breath is moving out, being with the breath as it moves into your body and out, binding your awareness to this process, to be present right now.

Silence (25 seconds)

⇒ And now the **third step**, is allowing your awareness to expand to the entire body, bringing a more spacious awareness to your experience, letting the breath be present but in the background.
Bringing attention to the entire length of the body from head to toe, including any tightness, tension or sensations related to holding on or bracing.
In this moment holding your awareness in this
⇒ spaciousness place, breathing in and breathing out. As you are breathing out allowing any tension, tightness or holding on or bracing sensations to leave with the breath

(Silence)

⇒ And when you are ready, opening your eyes, letting go of this brief practice.

Part 3

10 strategies to Transform your life

"You can't start the next chapter of your life if you keep re-reading the last one."

Unknown

Ask yourself…

◊ What does my life look like right now (in terms of my career, finances, relationships, health, spirituality, fitness etc)? Use 'Balance Your Life' see link below.

◊ How do I feel about my life? Am I happy with my life?

◊ What do I want my life to look like in 1 month… 6 months… 1 year?

◊ Does the way I am living my life, right now, align with how I want my life to look in 1 month… 6 months… 1 year?

◊ If not, why? What's getting in the way? What's holding me back?

◊ Am I willing to make changes in order to make them line up? Use 'Simplify Your Life' See link below.

⇒ For additional downloadable tools go to
https://www.viviennerawnsley.com/simplify-your-life/

⇒ Download, then complete the free pdfs
Simplify your Life and Balance your Life
⇒ For further support contact me via email

Become More Self Aware

One piece of advice when it comes to choosing to do things in a different way and worrying about the opinion of others; What people think of you – is none of your business.

Find what works for you. What feels right and gives you the life you want. That is your primary focus from now on.

We can pontificate and deliberate, avoid and ignore but deep down somewhere, if we give it space to speak, our intuition knows exactly what we need to do to change that feeling that life is happening to us, whilst we're standing by as a helpless bystander.

It is at the point we decide to choose 'THIS IS IT. NO MORE.' that things start to shift.

Rather than reach that point here are some questions to ask yourself daily that can help you become more self-aware.

◊   How am I feeling today?

◊   Am I Ok?

◊   Is how I am feeling affecting my physical and/or mental health?

◊   Am I making choices that support my wellbeing and future?

◊   Do I need guidance or support through anything?

Whether you answer yes or no to these questions they have given you something incredibly powerful – the power of choice.

◊ Do you continue to carry on in the same way hoping that somehow, someway things will change?

◊ Or do you choose to look at what your options are and make some different choices?

◊ Do you choose to stay in the same place or take action?

◊ Do you choose to do things the same or differently?

◊ Do you choose illbeing or wellbeing?

◊ Do you choose to do it alone or seek support?

Asking yourself these questions on a regular basis and acting on the answer will support you in making changes in your life.

Core beliefs

Without realising it most of us step into adult life with a set of core beliefs that rule our lives that we didn't ever choose. These beliefs were established way back when during the earliest years of our lives. Most of these beliefs were formed by the age of six or seven based on our thoughts about our experiences, the things that we see other people do and the things that are said to us.

As we get older these moulded patterns may work for us but equally, they may hold us back from making the choices and doing the things we would really like to do.

The great thing is that it is never too late to change.
Although NLP, Time Line Therapy and Hypnosis are amazing tools to use in supporting the change of beliefs at this deep level, here's one way to explore these beliefs for yourself.

Grab a pen and piece of paper then ask yourself these questions and see where it takes you.

⇒ What is my core belief around 'X'? (Choose a subject)

⇒ Is this my belief or one that I've inherited?

⇒ If it's inherited, what do I really believe? How does this make me feel?

⇒ If I acted from this new core belief, how would I be? Would I feel more like myself?

Start Living Differently

Knowing what you believe and living by those beliefs are two entirely different things. Deciding is easy. Putting them into practice, not so much. Especially when those around you have expectations, based on your previous beliefs about you and the world, that put demands on you.

Establishing boundaries that link to your new beliefs is one way to start living differently.

Maybe you were someone who believed that to be seen as a good person and to be accepted by others you needed to agree to their demands and became a 'yes' person. Perhaps your respect for yourself was so diminished that even when the requests demeaned who you are, you agreed feeling that your worth was so low it didn't matter anyway.

Setting boundaries that work for you, that maintain and regard you as the unique and precious individual that you are, is one way to support you in maintaining the beliefs you have discovered and stepping into the power of you.

Change your self-concept

It's always fascinated me how the New Zealand rugby team begin each overseas match with the Haka, a tradition that started way back in the 1800's.

In the same way that this 'war' cry is used by these sportsmen, we can create mantras to give ourselves the strength and the power to do all that we need to do and want to do each day.

Here is an A to Z of Enoughness to get you started:

I am Amazing enough
I am Brave enough
I am Confident enough
I am Decisive enough
I am Energised enough
I am Forgiving enough
I am Grateful enough
I am Happy enough
I am Intuitive enough
I am Joyous enough
I am Knowledgeable enough
I am Loveable enough
I am Magnificent enough
I am Noble enough
I am Optimistic enough
I am Powerful enough
I am Quintessential enough
I am Resilient enough
I am Strong enough
I am Thoughtful enough
I am Understanding enough
I am Vivacious enough
I am Wise enough
I am eXtraordinary enough
I am Youthful enough
I am Zealous enough

Affirmations, positive statements that can help you to challenge and overcome self-sabotaging and negative thoughts, can also be used in this way. When you repeat them often, and believe in them, you can start to make positive changes.

Some suggestions are:

I believe in, trust, and have confidence in myself.
I learn from my mistakes.
I forgive myself for not being perfect because I am human.
I am enough.
I love myself.
I believe I can be all I want to be.
I am worthy of my dreams.
I choose to be kind to myself and love myself unconditionally.
I have the freedom and the power to create the life I desire.

⇒ Create post its or notes in strategic places in your home or workplace – the mirror where you brush your teeth, the fridge door, your screen saver on your phone or lap top – and read them out loud to yourself, often.

Using these statements, together with accessing the energy points of the body - through the tapping technique of Emotional Freedom Technique (EFT), just like the amazing rugby players as they perform their pre match ritual, so can we master our lives and become all we choose to be.

Journaling

A daily practice method of journaling, called Morning Pages, can be regarded as the bedrock tool of a creative recovery. Morning Pages are three pages of longhand, stream of consciousness writing that Julia Cameron advocates to start each day. She recommends that these pages are written rather than word processed as through this activity the subconscious, unconscious parts of our thinking are accessed, explored, and resolved.

◊ They centre you and acting as a 'brain dump' clear your mind.

◊ They help to silence your biggest enemy – your very own inner dialogue, personal critic.

◊ They make you less anxious by getting stuff out and realising it's not as bad and scary as you though it was.

◊ They help to ground you in what is going on as opposed to what you've created as reality.

◊ They help you discover your creativity.

⇒ Choose a designated journaling book to record your thoughts in to reflect and observe your journey through.

⇒ Or use loose sheets of paper and once the writing is out discard it as exposed, explored and exhausted so no longer important on your journey to discovering you.

Change your Mood with Food

So often when we feel bad about ourselves or we are challenged in life we reach to food as a mood enhancer or suppressor.

Many of these habits are based in the stories of our past as we were rewarded with sweet treats when we did something that was good and to be proud of, or deprived food or treats when we misbehaved, disappointed or angered others.
Taking back control of our lives and putting ourselves as the person who makes the choices of what we eat and when we eat, can make a huge difference in how we feel about ourselves.

Knowing that we have choices and that we can make those choices freely, allows us to give ourselves the food and hydration that fuels our bodies and our minds to give us the outcomes we want.

Some things to remember are:

◊ Drink 2 to 2.5 litres of water a day—more during hot weather and whilst doing exercise

◊ Almonds are a great snack to lift your mood

◊ Eating a large portion of green vegetables at mealtimes will help to fill you, boost your metabolism and reduce your shape and size

◊ Avoid processed foods and cook from scratch when possible

◊ Reduce your caffeine and alcohol intake

◊ Berries, seeds and fruit are a great snacking alternative

◊ Dark chocolate contains less sugar than milk chocolate

Question your Thoughts

Often the thoughts that we have are just that, thoughts.

Yet when we continue to think the same thoughts, over time they become our reality.

One way to change our reality it to change the thoughts that we have about it.

⇒ Identify the automatic negative thought.
   'I'm worthless.' 'I'm useless.' 'What's wrong with me?'

⇒ Explore the cost of this automatic negative thought to you in your life.

⇒ Then define the opposite of this thought.
   'I'm enough.' 'I'm awesome.' 'I'm unique.'

⇒ What evidence is there of this positive replacement thought?

⇒ How do you feel when you believe this positive replacement thought?

⇒ Going back to the original automatic negative thought can you now say that it is categorically true?

⇒ What will you now choose to believe instead?

Gratitude

It has been demonstrated through scientific evidence that gratitude is good for our brains. The hypothalamus, a control centre in our brain that maintains balance in the systems in our bodies and wellbeing, is activated whenever we feel gratitude, pride, or do something altruistic for somebody else. That means gratitude actually makes our metabolism, hunger and other natural bodily functions work more smoothly.

Gratitude also increases our levels of resilience to stress, enables us to go to sleep better and experience more positive feelings.

Keeping track of elements of gratitude creates a go to place to support these outcomes.

⇒ Designate a special notebook

⇒ Write a list of 5 things you are grateful for each day

⇒ Start with small things

⇒ Expand to bigger things

⇒ Explore where those feelings of gratitude are in your body

⇒ What does gratitude feel like?

⇒ Use your list to support you on your more challenged days

Exercise in Nature

The benefits of exercise have been proven to increase our overall health, physically and mentally. More recently the ways that taking exercise in nature can impact on our lives has been explored.

Scientific studies have shown that 'green exercise' can improve self-esteem and mood, as well as reducing anxiety disorders and depression. It's not just the physiological effects of exercise, such as the release of endorphins, dopamine and serotonin that cause these responses. By comparing different exercise settings, studies showed that regular use of woods or parks for physical exercise reduced the risk of poor mental health, whereas no such pattern was found in non-natural settings like gyms.

Being in or near the natural world has also been proven to reduce stress and increase wellbeing, whether you're exercising or not. Simply having views of trees, plants and shrubs at work can increase employee wellbeing, and having the same views from a hospital window can decrease recovery time. So, combining nature and exercise is a great way to alleviate stress and overcome the feelings of boredom and additional exposure to technology that exercising inside a gym can result in.

Being outside in the sunshine when working out is a brilliant way to increase your vitamin D. Vitamin D boosts your immune system, helps fight depression, promotes bone growth and prevents osteoporosis, so it's an important vitamin to have.

Walking barefoot in nature to strengthen the immune system, improve sleep and reduce the risk of heart disease can be the simple act of walking to the recycling box at the bottom of your garden, walking along the beach feeling the pebbles and sand beneath your feet or striding through lush green grass.

Mindful thoughts, Meditation, Self-Hypnosis

In the busyness of life, we often find ourselves ruminating and chastising ourselves for events and experiences of the past or dreaming of a better life in the future. Yet the very moment we are in, the only time of our lives that we can actually guarantee will take place, is the present.

One of the best ways that we can pay attention to this present is to cultivate mindfulness, the act of being awake in the moment, connecting and 'befriending who we already are'.

Through meditation the muscle of our mind can expand who we are. Hypnosis allows us to develop further tools to explore the unconscious part of our mind and support us further in our journey of self-discovery.

Here's a short mindfulness meditation to use when you find your thoughts or moods spiralling in a negative direction.

⇒ First take a posture where your back is erect, but not stiff, letting the body express a sense of being present and awake.
⇒ Now, just with the body balanced where you are sitting, gently close your eyes and hold the body in awareness for this moment.
⇒ Just be aware of what the body is feeling.
⇒ Just present.
⇒ Noticing the entry and exit of the breath.
⇒ Not having to interfere with it, but just simply feeling it.
⇒ And if you're happy to, just simply drawing in a deep breath and letting it out slowly and gently.
⇒ Now just letting the breathing find its own rhythm.
⇒ If thoughts or feelings are arising, then just noticing them, not having to supress them, just observing them but preferring to let the attention rest with the breathing
⇒ So when you're ready, allowing the eyes to gently open and then mindfully move into whatever activities await you.

Part 4

A place for you to use for your own personal insights and reflections

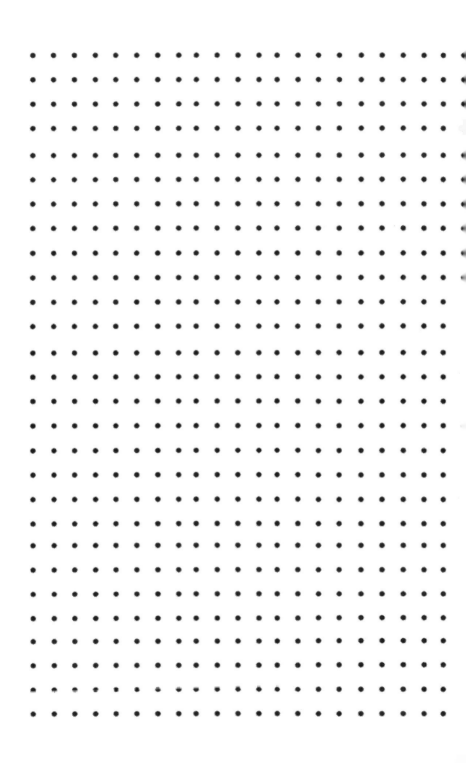

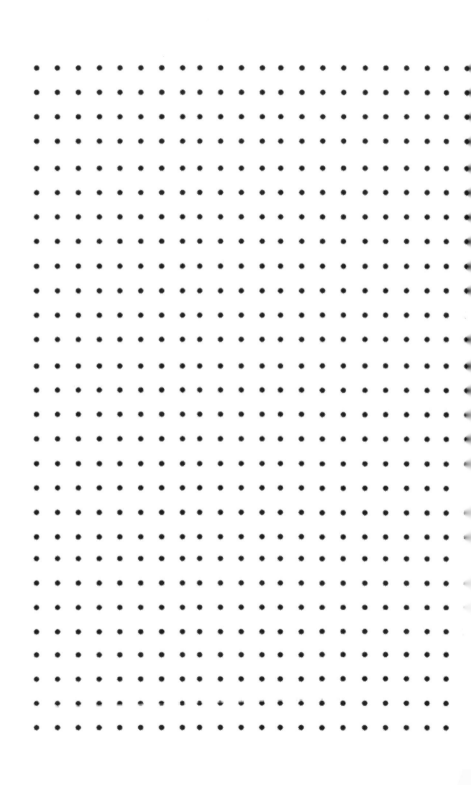

One final thought…

Use this mantra style of meditation to use to strengthen your personal power and increase your connection with others.

May I be happy
May I be healthy
May I ride the tides of my life
May I live in peace no matter what I am given

May you be happy
May you be healthy
May you ride the tides of your life
May you live in peace no matter what you are given

May we be happy
May we be healthy
May we ride the tides of our life
May we live in peace no matter what we are given

Printed in Great Britain
by Amazon